How d'ya like them Apples

MADGE BAIRD

GIBBS SMITH
TO ENRICH AND INSPIRE HUMANKIND

First Edition
20 19 18 17 16   5 4 3 2

Text © 2016 Madge Baird
Photographs © 2016 Susan Barnson Hayward

Published by
Gibbs Smith
P.O. Box 667
Layton, Utah 84041

1.800.835.4993 orders
www.gibbs-smith.com

Designed by Rita Sowins / Sowins Design and Sky Hatter
Food styling by Marcela Ferrinha
Food styling for Brown Sugar Apple Dumplings and Fruity Stuffing by Suzy Eaton
Prop styling by Annie Cheney

Printed and bound in Hong Kong
Gibbs Smith books are printed on paper produced from sustainable PEFC-certified forest/controlled wood source. Learn more at www.pefc.org.

Library of Congress Cataloging-in-Publication Data

Names: Baird, Madge, author.
Title: How d'ya like them apples / Madge Baird.
Other titles: How do you like them apples
Description: First edition. | Layton, Utah : Gibbs Smith, [2016] | Includes index.
Identifiers: LCCN 2016007408 | ISBN 9781423644446 [hardcover]
Subjects: LCSH: Cooking [Apples] | LCGFT: Cookbooks.
Classification: LCC TX813.A6 B352 2016 | DDC 641.6/411--dc23
LC record available at http://lccn.loc.gov/2016007408

CONTENTS

Introduction ... 7

Helpful Hints ... 8

Salads ... 9

Soups ... 25

Meats & Poultry ... 37

Pies & Pastries ... 71

Cakes, Cobblers, Breads & Sweet Treats ... 91

Index ... 126

Introduction

One of the great privileges of living in this day and time is the ready availability of fresh produce at farmers markets and grocery stores year-round. I say privilege, because we have access to much more variety now than we did just ten or fifteen years ago. It seems that supermarkets are really pumping up their produce sections. At one market I frequent, there is even a snack stand where parents can get complimentary apples, bananas, and oranges for their children to eat while they shop. It's a brilliant PR move.

During the past year, the variety of apples coming from farmers and through the produce distribution system has increased by about a third. Kiku is one of my new favorites for fresh eating: its flesh is crisp, juicy, and sweet. Gala is my go-to for salads and other dishes where they will be used raw. And Golden Delicious is my favorite pie-making apple.

But sometimes the apples in my pantry or cold storage don't get used up fast enough, and that means it's time for baking a luscious apple dessert or for adding more nutrition to a puréed soup or meat dish by coring and tucking in an apple or two. There are so many easy and delicious ways to use apples—right down to making applesauce of a few that might have started to wither—that there is no reason to waste an apple at all.

I hope you will find some favorite new recipes here. Let them inspire your cooking and enhance your enjoyment of this most versatile fruit.

Helpful Hints

1. About 7,500 varieties of apples are grown throughout the world. More than 2,500 varieties are grown in the United States and Canada.

2. Some varieties are better for baking than others. Pie apples should hold up and not become mushy when baked: neither should they remain crunchy. Granny Smith, Jonathan, Jonagold, Pink Lady, Golden Delicious, Rome, McIntosh, and Braeburn are a few good varieties for pies. The same varieties, plus many others, can be used for any of the recipes in this book where the apple is cooked. The fact is, all varieties will soften if cooked for a long enough time, but sometimes that would be longer than is good for the rest of the dish, such as the pie crust. The smaller the pieces of apple, the faster they cook.

3. Two pounds of apples make a 9-inch pie. There are two or three large apples in a pound.

4. To peel or not to peel? It's a matter of personal taste. Two-thirds of an apple's fiber is in the skin. The skin is high in antioxidants, and most of an apple's vitamin C content is just under the skin. Consider leaving the skin on when a recipe calls for grated or chopped apples.

5. Apples ripen or soften ten times faster at room temperature than when refrigerated.

6. Wrinkled apples, or those beyond their prime (but not spoiled), are ideal for making cobblers, cakes, soups, and applesauce.

7. A little lemon juice can wake up the flavor of bland apples for applesauce or in recipes.

Salads

SNAPPY
APPLE SALAD

Makes 4 servings

8 ounces sugar snap peas
2 green onions, thinly sliced
2 Granny Smith apples, cut into bite-size pieces
1 tablespoon chopped cilantro
$^1/_4$ cup sliced almonds
Sea salt, to taste
Freshly ground pepper, to taste
Juice of 1 lemon
2 tablespoons honey
2 tablespoons vegetable oil
Lettuce or arugula, optional

Rinse peas; trim and discard ends; slice on the diagonal into small pieces and place in a medium bowl. Add onions, apples, cilantro, and almonds. Season with salt and pepper.

In a small bowl, whisk together lemon juice, honey, and oil. Pour over salad ingredients and toss to coat. Serve on lettuce or arugula, if desired.

PISTACHIO, CHICKEN, AND APPLE SALAD

Makes 6 servings

2 cups diced crisp apples
1 cup diced celery
2 tablespoons finely diced red bell pepper
$^1/_2$ cup pistachio nuts
$1^1/_4$ cups diced grilled chicken
Salt, to taste
2 tablespoons French or Catalina dressing
$^1/_2$ cup mayonnaise
6 lettuce leaves or sandwich buns

Place apples, celery, bell pepper, nuts, and chicken in a medium bowl. Sprinkle with salt.

In a separate bowl, combine dressing and mayonnaise. Fold into the apple-chicken mixture until well coated. Serve on lettuce leaves or buns.

GRILLED CHICKEN, APPLE, AND LEEK SALAD

Makes 4 servings

2 medium apples, cored and cut into thin wedges
2 tablespoons melted butter or margarine
1 cup thinly sliced leek, white and green parts
2 tablespoons olive oil, divided
4 medium handfuls spinach leaves
1 large chicken breast, grilled and thinly sliced

Honey Vinaigrette

3 tablespoons fresh lemon juice
2 tablespoons honey
$^1/_3$ cup extra virgin olive oil
1 tablespoon chopped fresh herbs (parsley, tarragon, or thyme)
Salt, to taste
Pepper, to taste

Dip apple slices in butter and place in a hot frying pan or outdoor grill basket; cook for a little over 2 minutes per side, until apple begins to soften. Set aside. Grill sliced leeks in the same pan until wilted, about 10 minutes, using 1 tablespoon oil and any remaining butter; set aside.

Sauté spinach in remaining oil over high heat until wilted, tossing constantly. Reheat chicken in the grill pan. Assemble salads on 4 serving plates in the following order: spinach, leeks, apple, and chicken.

Honey Vinaigrette

Whisk lemon juice, honey, and oil together in a small bowl until emulsified and thickened. Add herbs and salt and pepper. Divide over salads.

BEET-APPLE SALAD

Makes 4 servings

Mixed salad greens
1 (15-ounce) can sliced beets, drained
2 medium-size green apples, sliced
1 (15-ounce) can garbanzo beans (chickpeas), drained and rinsed
Balsamic vinaigrette dressing
$1/3$ cup shredded Parmesan cheese

Assemble salads on 4 serving plates in the following order: greens, beets, apples, and beans. Spoon dressing lightly over salads and sprinkle with cheese.

APPLE-LINK
SALAD

Makes 4 servings

2 sweet crisp apples
8 maple-brown sugar sausage links
3 rounded tablespoons honey
1 tablespoon olive oil
2 teaspoons rice vinegar
1 (6-ounce) package fresh baby spinach

Core apples and cut into bite-size pieces.

In a medium frying pan, cook sausages on all 4 sides until well done. Cut each link into 3 lengths. Keep warm.

Place honey in a small bowl and heat in microwave until liquefied. Whisk in the oil and vinegar.

Divide spinach, apples, and sausages onto 4 serving plates. Spoon honey vinaigrette over the salads. Serve while sausages and vinaigrette are warm or at room temperature.

POTATO SALAD WITH BACON AND APPLES

Makes 8–10 servings

$^1/_2$ pound bacon, diced
5 medium-size red potatoes
3 large crisp red apples
$^1/_3$ cup chopped red onion
2 ribs celery, chopped
$^1/_3$ cup chopped yellow bell pepper
Salt and pepper, to taste

Honey Mustard Vinaigrette

$^1/_4$ cup apple cider vinegar
$^1/_2$ cup vegetable oil
1 tablespoon honey mustard
$^1/_4$ teaspoon ground red pepper
1 teaspoon thyme leaves

In a large frying pan, cook bacon until crisp; set aside.

Boil whole potatoes 30–40 minutes, until fork-tender, then drain and let cool. Peel and cube potatoes. Place in a large bowl.

Cut apples into chunks and add to potatoes. Add onion, celery, and bell pepper. Season with salt and pepper.

Honey Mustard Vinaigrette

In a separate bowl, whisk dressing ingredients together until emulsified. Pour dressing over salad and toss to coat.

O.J. FRUIT SALAD

Makes 4–6 servings

2 tablespoons Knox gelatin
1 cup boiling water
2 cups chopped apples
2 tablespoons lemon juice
2 oranges, segmented and cut bite size
1 cup pineapple tidbits, well drained
1 banana
2 cups orange juice, or a mix of orange and pineapple juices
$^1/_2$ cup sugar

In a small bowl, mix gelatin into water and let dissolve. In a large bowl, toss apples in lemon juice. Add oranges and pineapple and toss gently. Slice banana and distribute over the mixed fruit.

When gelatin has bloomed, mix it into the juice and add sugar. Stir to dissolve sugar. Transfer fruit to a mold, if desired. Carefully pour juice over the fruit. Refrigerate to set for at least 4 hours or overnight.

CURRY CHICKEN SALAD

Makes 4 servings

$1^1/4$ cups sliced grilled chicken
12 red grapes, halved
12 cherry tomatoes, halved
$1/3$ cup chopped celery
2 large Gala apples, diced
3 tablespoons light mayonnaise
2 tablespoons light Miracle Whip
$1^1/2$ teaspoons curry powder
2 teaspoons lemon juice
Salad greens or sandwich rolls

Place chicken, grapes, tomatoes, celery, and apples in a medium bowl. In a small bowl, whisk together the mayonnaise, Miracle Whip, curry powder, and lemon juice.

Pour dressing over chicken mixture and fold until well coated. Serve on a bed of salad greens or on sandwich rolls.

AUTUMN CHICKEN SALAD

Makes 4 servings

1¹/₄ cups diced cooked chicken
20 red grapes, halved
1 rib celery, chopped
2 medium red apples, cored and chopped
2 cups baby spinach leaves or arugula
¹/₃ cup roughly chopped pecans
¹/₃ cup mayonnaise
1 tablespoon crumbled blue cheese
1 tablespoon lemon juice
¹/₄ teaspoon salt
Salad greens or sandwich rolls

Place chicken, grapes, celery, apples, spinach, and pecans in a medium bowl. In a small bowl, whisk together the mayonnaise, cheese, lemon juice, and salt.

Pour dressing over chicken mixture and fold until well coated. Mound chicken salad on top of salad greens or serve on sandwich rolls.

CHICKEN QUESADILLAS WITH APPLES & BRIE

Makes 4 servings

2 teaspoons olive oil
$^1/_2$ cup thinly sliced leek, including white and tender green parts
2 large crisp sweet apples, cored and thinly sliced
2 teaspoons white balsamic or distilled vinegar
2 teaspoons demerara sugar*
$^1/_4$ teaspoon salt
$1^1/_4$ cups cubed Brie cheese
$1^1/_4$ cups roasted chicken, cut into small bite-size pieces
4 flour tortillas

Heat oil in large frying pan. Sauté leek over medium-high heat for 2 minutes, stirring once. Add apple slices and sauté until apple begins to soften (a little brown color adds flavor, but avoid burning). Sprinkle with vinegar, sugar, and salt.

Add cheese and chicken to frying pan. Cook over medium-low heat until cheese is melted and chicken is hot. Mix all ingredients together well and spoon onto center of warm tortillas; fold in half.

*1 teaspoon brown sugar can be substituted.

APPLE SLAW

2 cups shredded cabbage
2 cups shredded crisp red apples
$1/3$ cup light mayonnaise
1 tablespoon apple cider vinegar
$1/2$ teaspoon celery seed
$1/2$ teaspoon salt

Toss cabbage and apple in a medium bowl. In a separate bowl, whisk together the mayonnaise, vinegar, celery seed, and salt. Pour dressing over slaw and toss to coat. Serve chilled.

Soups

PUMPKIN-APPLE SOUP WITH BACON

Makes 6–10 servings

1/2 pound bacon, chopped
1 large onion, chopped
3 large cooking apples, peeled, cored, and chopped
1/8 teaspoon pepper
1/4 teaspoon cumin
4 teaspoons chicken bouillon powder
1/4 cup firmly packed brown sugar
1 cup water
2 cups apple juice
1 teaspoon apple cider vinegar
1/2 teaspoon liquid smoke
1 (29-ounce) can pumpkin purée, or 3 cups butternut squash purée

Cook bacon and onion in a large pot over medium-high heat for about 5 minutes, stirring occasionally. Scrape bottom of pan to loosen bacon bits. Reduce heat to medium. Add apples, pepper, and cumin; cover and cook for 5 minutes more, until onion begins to turn translucent and apples soften. Add bouillon, brown sugar, water, apple juice, vinegar, and liquid smoke. Bring to a boil then reduce heat and simmer for 5 minutes to finish cooking the apples. Stir in pumpkin, bring to a simmer again, and let cook for 5 minutes or longer while flavors meld. Serve hot.

VARIATION: For a vegetarian option, eliminate bacon and cook the onion and apples in 2 tablespoons canola oil instead. Substitute vegetable bouillon powder, increase liquid smoke to 1 teaspoon, and add 1 (14-ounce) can drained small white beans.

BEET AND APPLE SOUP

Makes 6–8 servings

1 tablespoon olive oil
1 teaspoon butter or margarine
2 cooking apples, peeled, cored, and thinly sliced
1 carrot, peeled and thinly sliced
1 stalk celery, thinly sliced
2 (14-ounce) cans beets, drained
1 cup apple juice
1 cup chicken broth
1 bay leaf
$^1/_2$ teaspoon salt
$^1/_4$ teaspoon freshly ground pepper
$^1/_2$ teaspoon chicken bouillon powder, optional
$^1/_4$ cup cream, optional

Heat oil and butter in a medium saucepan over medium heat. Place apples, carrot, and celery in pan and sauté, covered, until softened. Add beets, juice, broth, bay leaf, salt, and pepper. Bring to a low boil and cook, covered, for about 20 minutes while bay leaf infuses the broth.

Remove bay leaf. Purée soup with an immersion blender, or in batches with a blender or food processor. Heat through and taste; adjust seasoning with chicken bouillon as needed. If you prefer a mellower flavor, add cream.

Blender Caution

Hot food in a blender may explode, so stop the motor a couple of times and remove the lid to let the steam out, or remove the plug from the lid and cover the opening with a kitchen towel while blending.

BUTTERNUT-APPLE SOUP

Makes 6–8 servings

4 cups cooked mashed butternut squash*
1$^1/_2$ cups apple juice or cider
2–3 rounded teaspoons chicken bouillon powder
1 tablespoon dehydrated onion
$^1/_8$ teaspoon freshly ground pepper
$^1/_2$ cup fat-free half-and-half
Parmesan cheese, optional

Spray the bottom of a medium saucepan with oil. Place all ingredients in the pan, except half-and-half and Parmesan, and stir together. Bring soup to a boil over medium-high heat, stirring frequently. Reduce heat to low, cover, and let simmer until apples have softened, about 20 minutes. Stir frequently to prevent sticking.

Remove pan from heat. Blend soup to desired thickness with an immersion blender or in batches with a blender or food processor. Return to pan and stir in the half-and-half. Heat soup over medium until boiling. Remove from heat and ladle into bowls. Sprinkle lightly with cheese before serving.

*Start with squash purée, if you wish.

RED LENTIL SOUP WITH SWEET POTATO AND APPLE

Makes 6 servings

1 tablespoon olive oil
1 clove garlic, minced
1 small onion, chopped
$^3/_4$ cup red lentils, rinsed
4 cups chicken broth
1 sweet potato, peeled and thinly sliced
1 white potato, peeled and thinly sliced
3 medium apples, peeled and chopped
$^1/_2$ teaspoon cumin
$^1/_2$ teaspoon red chili powder
$^1/_2$ teaspoon paprika
1 teaspoon chicken bouillon powder
Salt, to taste
2 cups water, divided
$^1/_2$ cup evaporated milk, optional

In a medium saucepan, heat oil and sauté garlic and onion over medium heat until onion turns translucent, about 7 minutes. Add lentils and broth; bring to a boil, reduce heat, and simmer for 15 minutes. Add the sweet and white potatoes, apples, cumin, chili powder, paprika, chicken bouillon, and salt; add enough water to cover the vegetables. Cover and simmer until potatoes have softened, about 20 minutes.

Remove pan from heat and purée contents with an immersion blender, or in batches with a blender or food processor. If too thick to purée effectively, add a little more water. Add milk, taste, and adjust seasonings as needed.

CURRIED CARROT-APPLE BISQUE

Makes 4 servings

5 medium carrots, peeled and sliced into coins
1 rib celery, sliced
3 medium cooking apples, peeled and sliced
1 tablespoon dehydrated chopped onion
1 tablespoon chicken bouillon powder
$1/2$ teaspoon curry powder
$1/4$ teaspoon marjoram
$1/4$ teaspoon dried thyme leaves
$1/4$ teaspoon freshly ground pepper
$1/8$ teaspoon paprika
$1/2$ cup water
$1/2$ cup cream or coconut milk

Place all ingredients except cream in a medium saucepan; cover and bring to a boil. Reduce heat to simmer and cook for 20–25 minutes, until vegetables are tender. Using an immersion blender, blender, or food processor, blend cooked vegetables in their liquid to desired consistency; add cream and reheat.

CREAMY PARSNIP AND APPLE SOUP

Makes 4 servings

1 small onion, chopped
1 tablespoon butter or margarine
1 tablespoon olive oil
2 sweet-tart apples (such as Gala or Granny Smith), peeled and chopped
1 $^1/_4$ pounds parsnips, peeled and chopped
3 cups water
1 tablespoon chicken bouillon powder
1 tablespoon freshly squeezed lemon juice
1 teaspoon salt
$^1/_2$ teaspoon cinnamon
$^1/_2$ teaspoon nutmeg
1 cup cream
1 cup milk
1 tablespoon cornstarch mixed with 2 tablespoons water, optional

In a large saucepan, sauté onion in butter and oil over medium heat for 3 minutes. Add apples and sauté for 3–4 minutes more. Add parsnips, water, bouillon, lemon juice, salt, cinnamon, and nutmeg. Cover and bring to a boil; reduce heat and simmer for 20 minutes, until parsnips are tender. Remove from heat and let cool.

Purée soup with an immersion blender, blender, or food processor. Stir in cream and milk. Return saucepan to heat until just boiling, stirring frequently. If soup is too thin, stir in cornstarch mixture to thicken.

NOTE: You can convert this recipe to vegetarian by substituting vegetable bouillon powder and reducing onion to 1/2 cup.

PIMENTO CREAM SOUP

1 (10-ounce) bag fresh vegetable medley (broccoli, carrot, and cauliflower)
2 cooking apples, peeled, cored, and thinly sliced
1 teaspoon seasoned salt
$^1/_2$ teaspoon salt
1 teaspoon dried thyme leaves
$1^1/_4$ cups water
1 (5-ounce) jar Kraft Pimento Cheese Spread
1 cup milk

In a medium saucepan, combine vegetables, apples, seasoned salt, salt, and thyme. Add the water and cook over medium-high heat until vegetables are tender. Stir in cheese to melt. Purée soup with an immersion blender, blender, or food processor. Add milk and continue blending until mixed.

CABBAGE AND APPLE SOUP

Makes 6–8 servings

1 pound ground beef
1 small onion, chopped
$1/3$ cup chopped bell pepper (red or green), optional
2 medium potatoes, chopped
$1/2$ head green cabbage (about 1 pound), cored and chopped
3 crisp apples, chopped
4 cups water
3 beef bouillon cubes
Salt and freshly ground pepper, to taste

In a large saucepan, brown ground beef, onion, and bell pepper. Drain excess grease. Add potatoes, cabbage, apples, water, and bouillon cubes; cover with a lid and bring to a boil. Reduce to simmer for 35–40 minutes, until vegetables are cooked. Taste and season with salt and pepper.

NOTE: This recipe was inspired by my friend Florene McCrary.

Meats & Poultry

DRESSED-UP PORK MEDALLIONS

Makes 4 servings

4 tablespoons olive oil, divided
2 large sweet onions, sliced $^1/_4$ inch thick, rings separated
2 large sweet apples, peeled, cored, and cut into 12–16 wedges each
12 ($^3/_8$-inch-thick) slices pork tenderloin
2 teaspoons Worcestershire sauce
Salt and freshly ground pepper, to taste
2 teaspoons vinegar or freshly squeezed lemon juice
1 pound mushrooms, thickly sliced
1 tablespoon butter or margarine

In a large, deep frying pan, heat 2 tablespoons oil over medium heat. Cook onion rings, stirring occasionally, until they have turned golden, about 20 minutes. Transfer onions to a bowl and set aside. Raise heat to medium high and add 1 tablespoon oil. Cook apples until they soften or begin to turn golden, about 10 minutes, turning occasionally. Transfer apple slices to a bowl and set aside.

Preheat oven to lowest temperature. Heat remaining oil in the same frying pan and place pork medallions flat on bottom of the pan (cook in batches if necessary). Sprinkle lightly with Worcestershire sauce and season with salt and pepper. Cook over medium-high heat until browned on both sides. Transfer to a warm oven.

Deglaze frying pan with vinegar. Cook mushrooms in butter over medium-high heat, stirring frequently, until they begin to turn golden brown. Add reserved onions and apples to reheat. Season with salt and pepper. Serve pork medallions with vegetable-apple medley on the side. Spoon any juices remaining in the pan over the meat.

FULL-MEAL OVEN ROAST

Makes 8–10 servings

4 medium baking potatoes, peeled and halved
8 large carrots, peeled and cut into large pieces
1 (2–3 pound) cross rib beef roast or other pot roast
2 medium onions, quartered
1 (14-ounce) can beef broth
1^1/$_2$ teaspoons salt, divided
1 teaspoon freshly ground pepper
2 turnips, peeled and cut into thirds
4 apples, cored and halved
16 Brussels sprouts
^{1}/$_2$ cup flour
^{3}/$_4$ cup water
^{1}/$_2$ teaspoon beef bouillon powder

Preheat oven to 325 degrees. Spray a large Dutch oven or covered baking dish with olive oil. Place potatoes and carrots in bottom of pan. Set beef on vegetables and top with onions. Pour broth over the meat. Sprinkle with 1 teaspoon salt and the pepper. Cover tightly and bake for 2 hours. Remove roast from oven.

Place turnips, apples, and Brussels sprouts around the roast and sprinkle with remaining salt. Return covered pan to oven and bake for 1–1 ½ hours, until a fork inserts easily into the meat.

To make gravy, pour pan drippings into a small saucepan over medium high. Whisk the flour into the water then whisk into the drippings along with bouillon. Bring to a boil and simmer for about 2 minutes, stirring constantly. Slice meat and serve with vegetables and gravy.

SUNDAY
DUTCH OVEN PORK

Makes 4 servings

4 medium potatoes
6 carrots, peeled
1 medium yellow onion, peeled and quartered
4 sweet-tart apples (such as Gala or Granny Smith), cored and halved
Salt and freshly ground pepper, to taste
4 ($1/2$-to $3/4$-inch-thick) pork chops or boneless ribs
1 tablespoon Southwestern or Mexican spice blend (salt, garlic, onion,
     red pepper, and smoked paprika)

Preheat oven to 350 degrees. Spray a Dutch oven or covered baking dish with olive oil. Place potatoes, carrots, onion, and apples in the pan; spread evenly and sprinkle with salt and pepper.

Rub pork on all sides with spice blend and place on top of vegetables. Cover and cook for 1 1/2 hours; then test to see if meat is fork-tender. If not, cover and cook for 30 minutes more and test again. Cook longer, if needed. For the last 20 minutes of cooking, remove lid and allow meat to brown.

SLOW-COOKER APPLE CIDER POT ROAST

Makes 6–8 servings

2 tablespoons olive oil
1 (3-pound) lean chuck roast
3–4 cups apple cider
2 teaspoons beef bouillon granules
1 large onion, peeled and cut into wedges
4 large carrots, peeled and cut into chunks
2–3 apples, peeled, cored, and quartered
1 clove garlic, chopped
1 bay leaf
1 teaspoon salt

Heat oil over medium-high heat in a frying pan large enough to hold the roast. Brown meat on both sides, and then transfer to a 4-quart or larger slow cooker. Pour in cider nearly to top of meat, but do not cover.

Sprinkle bouillon into liquid and stir to mix. Arrange onion, carrots, apples, and garlic on top of meat. Tuck the bay leaf into the liquid. Sprinkle with salt. Cook on high for 1 hour then on low for 6–8 hours or overnight, until meat can be pulled apart with a fork.

PORK CHOPS WITH SAUTÉED APPLES

Makes 4 servings

4 tablespoons oil, divided
4 bone-in or 8 boneless thin-cut pork chops
Salt and freshly ground pepper, to taste
1 tablespoon rice vinegar
2 tablespoons butter or margarine
4–6 apples, peeled, cored, and sliced
1 tablespoon honey mustard, plus more to taste

In a large frying pan, heat 2 tablespoons oil over medium-high heat. Season both sides of each chop with salt and pepper. Fry pork chops in batches on both sides until browned and cooked through. Add remaining oil, if needed. Remove from pan and cover cooked chops with foil to keep warm while cooking apples.

Deglaze the frying pan with vinegar. Spread butter and apples evenly over the bottom of the pan. Cook on medium high about 12 minutes, turning frequently, or until apples start to soften. (If apples are not getting tender, add a little water and cover the pan with a lid for a few minutes to let the apples steam; then remove the lid and let the water evaporate.) When apples are soft, stir in mustard and sprinkle with a little salt. Taste and adjust seasoning with salt or mustard to your liking. Serve the pork chops with apples on the side.

APPLE-STUFFED CHICKEN BREASTS

Makes 2–4 servings

2 boneless, skinless chicken breasts, well rinsed and dried
3 tablespoons Boursin garlic and herb cheese, room temperature
1 baking apple, cored, peeled and cut into 8 wedges
2 kale leaves, torn and tough stems removed
Salt and freshly ground pepper, to taste

Preheat oven to 350 degrees.

Spray the bottom of an 8 x 8-inch baking dish with cooking oil.

Pound each chicken breast between 2 layers of plastic wrap to ½ inch thick. Divide the cheese evenly and spread on half of each chicken breast. Place 4 apple wedges over cheese and top with kale. Fold other half of chicken breast over the top and sprinkle lightly with salt and pepper.

Place the chicken into the prepared baking dish. Cover tightly with foil and bake for 40 minutes; remove foil and test for doneness. If chicken is not cooked through, continue cooking for 5–10 minutes until done. Spoon any pan juices over the top to moisten chicken.

TURKEY MEATBALLS WITH APPLE-DIJON GLAZE

Makes 30 meatballs

$^3/_4$ cup fine bread crumbs

2 teaspoons cornstarch

1 tablespoon all-purpose flour

$^3/_4$ pound ground turkey or chicken

$1^1/_2$ cups finely grated apple

1 teaspoon salt

1 teaspoon seasoned salt

1 tablespoon sage

$^1/_2$ teaspoon dried thyme leaves

$^1/_2$ teaspoon paprika

1 egg

$^3/_4$ cup apple jelly

1 teaspoon creamy Dijon mustard

1 teaspoon rice vinegar

Preheat oven to 400 degrees. Line a baking sheet with a silicone mat or wax paper sprayed with cooking oil.

In a small bowl, mix bread crumbs, cornstarch, and flour together. Place turkey, apple, salt, seasoned salt, sage, thyme, paprika, and egg in a medium bowl and add bread crumbs. Mix until well combined. Roll into ¾-inch balls and place on baking sheet. Bake for 20 minutes.

Combine jelly, mustard, and vinegar in a large saucepan over medium heat; stir until smooth. Remove meatballs from oven, transfer to the hot glaze and stir to cover. Using a slotted spoon, move meatballs back to the baking sheet and bake for 5 minutes. Repeat the process and bake for 3 minutes more. Serve with any remaining sauce for dipping. Cooked, glazed meatballs can be frozen in an airtight container for later use.

MINI TURKEY MEATLOAVES

Makes 12 meatloaves

Meatloaf

1 pound ground turkey (97 percent lean)
$1/4$ pound ground pork
1 small onion, finely chopped
2 cups finely chopped apples
1 rib celery, finely chopped
$1 1/2$ cups fine bread crumbs
$1/2$ cup raisins, softened
$1 1/2$ teaspoons sage
$1/2$ teaspoon dried thyme leaves
$1/2$ teaspoon marjoram
$1 1/2$ teaspoons salt
1 (8-ounce) can tomato sauce
2 eggs

Sauce

$1/2$ cup ketchup
1 teaspoon Dijon mustard
1 teaspoon apple cider vinegar
1 tablespoon brown sugar

Preheat oven to 350 degrees. Place all the meatloaf ingredients into a large bowl in the order listed and combine until well incorporated. Spray the cups of a 12-cup muffin tin with cooking oil. Fill each muffin cup with meatloaf mixture to the top of the tin.

Mix sauce ingredients in a small bowl, and spoon over tops of the meatloaves. Place the tin on a baking sheet and bake for 40–45 minutes. Turn off heat and let rest in the oven for 15 minutes while a thin crust forms.

Savory Mains & Sides

SWEET-AND-SOUR CABBAGE AND APPLE SKILLET

Makes 8–12 servings

4 tablespoons butter or margarine
3 tablespoons dehydrated onion
$1^1/_2$–2 pounds red cabbage, thinly sliced and chopped
1 teaspoon ground cloves
2 teaspoons ground allspice
2 teaspoons salt
1 cup firmly packed brown sugar
$^1/_4$ cup red wine vinegar
$^3/_4$ cup hot water
6 tart apples, cored and chopped

In a large frying pan, melt butter and sauté the onion until it begins to brown. Add cabbage and toss with onion. Add cloves, allspice, salt, brown sugar, and vinegar; toss and add water. Cover pan with a lid and let mixture simmer and steam for 30 minutes, stirring occasionally. Mix in apples. Cover and continue cooking for about 20 minutes more, until cabbage and apples are tender. Remove lid and taste; adjust sugar and spices to your liking. Continue simmering, uncovered, to cook off the liquid in the bottom of pan. Serve warm. This dish will keep in the refrigerator for about 1 week.

SWEET POTATO, ORANGE, AND APPLE BAKE

Makes 6–8 servings

1 large sweet potato, peeled
3 apples, peeled, cored, and thinly sliced
1 teaspoon salt, divided
$^3/_4$ cup apple juice
Juice and zest of 1 orange
$^1/_3$ cup roughly chopped pecans, optional
$^1/_3$ cup raisins, optional
$^1/_3$ cup firmly packed brown sugar
2 teaspoons cornstarch
$^1/_2$ teaspoon cinnamon
$^1/_8$ teaspoon nutmeg
Mini marshmallows, optional

Preheat oven to 350 degrees. Spray an 8 x 10-inch baking dish with cooking oil.

Slice sweet potato into rounds and then half-rounds. In a large saucepan, parboil potatoes about 10 minutes, just until they begin to soften; drain. Layer potatoes with apples in baking dish and sprinkle with ½ teaspoon salt.

In a medium saucepan, combine apple and orange juices, zest, pecans, raisins, remaining salt, brown sugar, cornstarch, cinnamon, and nutmeg. Cook over medium-high heat, whisking frequently, until juice begins to thicken. Pour sauce over sweet potatoes and apples. Cover dish tightly with foil and bake for about 35 minutes, until apples and sweet potatoes are soft. Remove foil after 20 minutes, distribute marshmallows over top, and continue baking until done.

WARM FIVE-SPICE APPLE SLAW

Makes 4 servings

2 tablespoons canola oil
$^1/_2$ teaspoon sesame oil
2 cups thinly sliced and chopped green cabbage
2 medium-size tart apples, cored and cut into matchsticks
2 tablespoons diced red onion
$1^1/_2$ teaspoons Chinese five-spice powder
1 tablespoon hoisin sauce
$^1/_4$ teaspoon salt

In a large frying pan, heat oils over medium heat. Toss remaining ingredients together in a large bowl. Transfer vegetable mixture to the hot frying pan and sauté, stirring frequently, for 5–7 minutes, just until vegetables begin to brown but are still crunchy. Increase heat to medium high, if needed; do not leave unattended. Serve warm as a side to meats or poultry.

VEGETABLE AND APPLE CURRY

Makes 8 servings

1 large or 2 medium Yukon Gold potatoes, peeled and cut into small cubes
1 large onion, cut into 10–12 wedges and separated
2 cloves garlic, minced
2 tablespoons seeded and minced hot chile pepper (such as jalapeño or Anaheim)
3 sweet-tart apples, cored and roughly chopped
2–3 tablespoons canola or olive oil
$^3/_4$ cup golden raisins
2–3 cups frozen peas
2 tablespoons curry powder, plus more to taste
Salt and freshly ground pepper, to taste
1 (14-ounce) can coconut milk
2 teaspoons cornstarch dissolved in 1 tablespoon water, optional

Place potatoes in a large saucepan and add enough water to nearly cover. Boil potatoes over medium-high heat just until tender, about 20 minutes. In a large, deep frying pan, sauté onion, garlic, chile pepper, and apples in oil over medium to medium-high heat for 12–15 minutes, until onion is translucent; stir frequently.

Drain potatoes and add to frying pan, along with raisins and peas. Add curry powder and season with salt and pepper. Stir to combine. Pour in coconut milk and stir. Continue to cook for 15–20 minutes, stirring frequently. A mixture of cornstarch and water may be used to thicken the sauce, if desired. Taste and adjust seasonings to as needed.

SPINACH-APPLE SAUTÉ

Makes 2-4 servings

1 tablespoon canola oil
$^1/_3$ cup raisins
1 garlic clove, minced
$^1/_2$ cup pine nuts, pumpkin seeds, or raw cashews
2 crisp, sweet apples (such as Gala), cored and chopped into small pieces
$^1/_4$-$^1/_3$ cup cooked mild Italian ground sausage
1 (6-ounce) package fresh baby spinach
2 teaspoons shredded Parmesan cheese, optional

Heat oil over medium heat in a large frying pan. Sauté raisins, garlic, and nuts until garlic is cooked but not browned. Add apple and sauté until softened, stirring frequently, about 5 minutes. Add sausage to reheat. Add spinach leaves and toss until spinach is slightly wilted but still bright green. Sprinkle with Parmesan.

PARMESAN ROASTED APPLE-VEGETABLE MEDLEY

Makes 8 servings

2 large, firm apples, cored and thickly sliced
1 medium onion, cut into 8 wedges, layers separated
6 carrots, peeled and halved vertically
2 parsnips, peeled and sliced
$1/2$ pound Brussels sprouts, halved
1 small butternut squash, peeled, seeded, and thinly sliced
1 fennel bulb, thinly sliced and separated
$1/4$ cup extra virgin olive oil
$3/4$ cup grated Parmesan cheese

Preheat oven to 450 degrees. Spray a large baking sheet with cooking oil.

Place apples and vegetables in a large bowl and toss with olive oil and Parmesan. Transfer to prepared baking sheet and bake, uncovered, for 35–40 minutes, turning every 10 minutes or so. Remove from the oven when done to your liking (I prefer to develop some browning/caramelization).

SAVORY SAUSAGE-AND-APPLE RICE STUFFING

Makes 4-6 servings

2 acorn squash
1 cup uncooked long-grain and wild rice
$^1/_2$ teaspoon salt
$^1/_4$ teaspoon thyme leaves
2 cups chicken or vegetable broth
2 sweet-tart apples (such as Gala or Granny Smith), chopped
$^1/_3$ cup chopped onion
$^1/_2$ cup cooked ground sausage
$^1/_4$ teaspoon freshly ground pepper
$^1/_4$ cup apple juice or cider

Preheat oven to 375 degrees.

Cut squash in half and remove seeds. Spray the cut edges of the squash with olive oil.

In a medium saucepan, cook rice, salt, and thyme in broth according to package directions. When done, mix in apple, onion, sausage, and pepper.

Place squash halves cut side up on a baking sheet or in a Dutch oven. Fill cavities of squash with the rice mixture. Pour about 2 tablespoons apple cider over the rice in each half. Cover squash tightly with foil, or cover Dutch oven with a lid.

Bake for 1 hour, or until a fork can be easily inserted into the thickest part of the squash.

SAUSAGE AND APPLE PASTA

Makes 8 servings

3/4 pound link breakfast sausage
1 leek, white and tender green parts, chopped
4 Golden Delicious apples, cored and sliced
1 tablespoon olive oil
2 tablespoons butter or margarine
1 teaspoon bacon fat
Salt and freshly ground pepper, to taste
2 teaspoons apple cider vinegar
1/4 cup water
1 (10-ounce) package fresh baby spinach
1 cup heavy cream
1/2 cup grated Parmesan cheese
1 pound penne pasta, cooked al dente and drained

In a deep frying pan or large saucepan, brown sausage on all sides and cook through; drain grease. Let sausage cool a bit then cut each link into 4 pieces.

In the same pan, sauté the leek and apples together in oil, butter, and bacon fat until apples begin to soften. Sprinkle lightly with salt and pepper. Return sausage to the pan then add the vinegar and water. Add spinach, sprinkle with about 1 teaspoon salt, cover pan with lid, and cook on medium heat for about 5 minutes, tossing a couple of times, until spinach wilts. Add cream and Parmesan and toss. Add cooked pasta and toss to coat. Cover and heat until warmed through.

STIR-FRIED VEGETABLES WITH HOISIN

Makes 4 servings

10 Brussels sprouts
2 large carrots
2 Granny Smith apples
2 tablespoons olive oil
1 clove garlic, minced
2 tablespoons hoisin sauce
Salt and freshly ground pepper, to taste

Clean and slice the Brussels sprouts and carrots very thinly. Core apples and slice very thinly then slice crosswise into matchsticks.

Heat oil in a frying pan over medium heat; add garlic and cook for 1 minute. Add prepared vegetables and apples and stir-fry for about 2 minutes. Clear a spot in the frying pan to add hoisin. Stir to heat then mix with the vegetables to coat. Sprinkle with salt and pepper. Continue cooking until vegetables are crisp-tender, about 3 minutes.

OVERNIGHT BREAKFAST CASSEROLE

Makes 8–10 servings

6 cups torn day-old bread
4 apples,* chopped (about 4 cups)
1¹/4 pounds ground country sausage, broken into small pieces
Salt, to taste
8 eggs
2 teaspoons sage powder
4 cups milk
Freshly ground pepper, to taste

Spray a 9 x 13-inch baking dish with cooking oil. Layer bread, apples, and sausage evenly in the dish. Sprinkle with salt.

In a medium bowl, lightly beat the eggs with sage; then whisk in milk. Season egg mixture with salt and pepper and carefully pour over the bread. Press bread into milk to moisten it. Cover dish tightly with foil and refrigerate overnight.

When ready to bake, preheat oven to 350 degrees. Bake, uncovered, for 45–50 minutes, until center of the casserole is cooked and a knife inserted in the middle comes out clean. If bread is browning too much toward the end of baking time, cover loosely with foil.

*This is a good use for apples beyond their prime.

NOTE: This recipe was inspired by my friend Nathalie Dupree.

POTATO-APPLE GRATIN WITH HAM

Makes 4–6 servings

1 (6–8 ounces) package au gratin potatoes*
4 large Granny Smith apples, peeled and diced
1 cup diced ham
2 tablespoons butter or margarine
$1^3/_4$ cups boiling water
1 cup milk
$^1/_3$ cup grated cheddar cheese

Preheat oven to 400 degrees. Spray a 2-quart or larger casserole dish with cooking oil. Spread dehydrated potato slices in bottom of casserole dish. Layer apples and ham over potatoes.

In a medium bowl, combine butter with boiling water and let butter melt; add milk and packet of powdered cheese and stir well. Pour milk mixture over the contents of the casserole dish. Be sure all potatoes are covered. Bake, uncovered, for 25 minutes. Remove casserole from oven and sprinkle with grated cheese. Return casserole to oven for 10 minutes, or until liquid has been absorbed and the cheese sauce is creamy.

*Boxed, dehydrated form. Name brands and store brands work equally well.

BAKED BEANS
WITH APPLE

Makes 6–8 servings

2 (15-ounce) cans white beans
3–4 crisp sweet apples, cored and cut into $^1/_2$-inch chunks
$^1/_4$ cup diced uncooked bacon
2 tablespoons apple cider vinegar
$^1/_2$ cup firmly packed brown sugar
1 (6-ounce) can tomato paste
1 teaspoon bacon fat, optional
$^1/_2$ teaspoon liquid smoke
Salt, to taste
Freshly ground pepper, to taste

Preheat oven to 350 degrees. Spray a medium baking dish with cooking oil.

Transfer beans and about half of their liquid to a medium bowl. Add apples and bacon.

In a separate small bowl, combine vinegar, brown sugar, tomato paste, bacon fat, and liquid smoke. Stir tomato mixture into beans. Season with salt and pepper. Transfer mixture to prepared baking dish. Cover and cook for 1–1 ½ hours. Serve hot or cold. This dish is even better the next day.

APPLE-STUFFED ACORN SQUASH

Makes 2-4 servings

1 acorn squash
1 teaspoon butter or margarine
1 large apple, chopped
1 tablespoon raisins
2 tablespoons brown sugar
2 tablespoons orange juice

Preheat oven to 400 degrees. Spray a baking sheet with cooking oil.

Halve squash and remove seeds. Bake both halves cut side down on the baking sheet for 20 minutes. Remove from oven and lower temperature to 350 degrees.

Turn squash face up and lightly run butter over cut edges to prevent drying out. Divide apple and raisins between the 2 halves and fill the cavities. Mix brown sugar with orange juice and pour over the apples in each half. Cover squash lightly with foil and return to oven until done, about 35 minutes. Total cooking time will vary according to the size and thickness of the squash. Squash is done when a fork can be easily inserted into the flesh.

FRUITY STUFFING

Makes about 15 servings

1¹/2 medium loaves bread, torn and dried
1 medium onion, finely chopped
2 large red apples, cored and cut into chunks
3 ribs celery, thinly sliced
¹/2 cup craisins, softened
2 teaspoons chicken bouillon powder
2 tablespoons poultry seasoning
2–3 cups hot water

Preheat oven to 350 degrees.

Line a 9 x 13-inch baking dish with heavy-duty foil, allowing about 8 inches overhang on both long sides. Spray the inside and overhanging foil lightly with cooking oil.

Place all ingredients except water in a large bowl and toss to distribute seasonings. Pour in the water, 1 cup at a time, and mix to moisten the bread mixture. If you prefer moister stuffing, add all the water and possibly more until it is moistened to your liking. Keep in mind that the apples will add moisture as they cook.

Transfer stuffing to the lined baking dish and distribute evenly. Fold sides of foil over the top and seal the ends. Bake for about 1 ½–2 hours, until the bottom and edges turn brown but not burned. Carefully open and fold back the foil. Return to the oven and bake for another 10–15 minutes to brown the top of the stuffing.

COMPANY PILAF

Makes 6 cups

6 tablespoons butter or margarine
1 1/2 cups Uncle Ben's Original Converted Rice
2 (14.5-ounce) cans chicken broth
1/2 cup water
6 tablespoons freshly squeezed lemon juice
Salt and freshly ground pepper, to taste
4 tablespoons olive oil, divided
1 leek, white and tender green parts, cleaned and diced
3 medium-size tart apples (such as Pink Lady, Granny Smith, Gala, or Cameo), cored and chopped
1/2 cup slivered almonds

In a medium saucepan, melt butter over medium heat. Stir in rice, increase heat to medium high, and let rice sauté in butter until grains start turning golden brown. Stir frequently to prevent burning. Pour in broth, water, and juice; season with salt and pepper. Cover and simmer about 20 minutes, until grains are soft to the tooth.

Heat 2 tablespoons of oil in a large frying pan and sauté leek over medium heat until it wilts, about 8 minutes; remove and set aside. Add remaining oil and the apples. Sauté over medium-high heat, stirring until apples begin to brown. Remove from heat. When rice is done, remove from heat and mix in the leek, apples, and almonds.

Pies & Pastries

CINNAMON CRUMBLE APPLE PIE

Makes 6–8 servings

1 (9-inch) unbaked pie crust
6–8 cooking apples
2 teaspoons freshly squeezed lemon juice
$^3/_4$ cup sugar
$^1/_2$ teaspoon cinnamon
$^1/_2$ teaspoon nutmeg
1 tablespoon cornstarch
$^1/_2$ teaspoon salt

Cinnamon Crumble Topping

$^3/_4$ cup all-purpose flour
$^3/_4$ cup sugar
$^1/_4$ teaspoon cinnamon
6 tablespoons melted butter or margarine

Preheat oven to 425 degrees. Place pie crust into a pie pan; trim and crimp edges. Peel and core the apples. Slice apples into a large bowl until you have 5–6 cups. Sprinkle with lemon juice and toss. In a small bowl, stir together sugar, cinnamon, nutmeg, cornstarch, and salt. Sprinkle sugar mixture over the apples and toss to coat. Let sit for 10–15 minutes while the juice starts to come out of the apples.

For the topping, mix flour, sugar, and cinnamon in a medium bowl. Add butter and mix to moisten. Transfer apple slices with juice to the pie pan. Leave the center slightly higher than the sides, with no apples overlapping the rim. Spread topping evenly over top. Bake in the center of the oven for 40–45 minutes, until apples are cooked and topping is lightly browned.

CLASSIC DOUBLE-CRUST APPLE PIE

Makes 6–8 servings

2 (8- or 9-inch) unbaked pie crusts
6 cups peeled and sliced cooking apples
Juice of $^1/_2$ lemon
$^3/_4$ cup plus 2 teaspoons sugar, divided
1 teaspoon cinnamon
$^1/_2$ teaspoon nutmeg
2 tablespoons all-purpose flour

Preheat oven to 400 degrees. Place 1 pie crust into a pie pan.

Place apples in a large bowl, sprinkle with lemon juice and toss. Combine $^3/_4$ cup sugar, cinnamon, nutmeg, and flour; toss with apples.

Spread apples in pie crust and arrange so they mound in the middle and are lower than the edge of the pan around the outside. Brush edges of the crust with water. Position other pie crust over apples, overlapping the edge of the bottom crust. Press top and bottom crusts together. Trim any overhanging crust with a knife; flute the edge or crimp with a fork. Cut 3 short slits in top crust to vent. Sprinkle remaining sugar over top of pie crust.

Place pie on a baking sheet and bake in center or just above center of the oven for 50 minutes. If crust gets too brown around edges before pie is finished cooking, cover loosely with foil. Let cool before slicing, as crust will hold up better when it is cool.

MINI APPLE DUMPLINGS WITH GINGER ALE

Makes 8 servings

2 medium baking apples, peeled, cored, and quartered
1 can refrigerated crescent rolls
4 tablespoons brown sugar
4 tablespoons melted butter or margarine
1 (12-ounce) can ginger ale

Preheat oven to 375 degrees. Spray an 8 x 8-inch baking dish with cooking oil.

Separate crescent dough into 8 triangles. Starting from the wide end, wrap 1 triangle of dough around each piece of apple, pinching dough together to seal. Place mini dumplings in baking dish; do not allow to touch. Sprinkle with brown sugar and pour butter over top. Pour ginger ale around the edges and between the dumplings. Bake for about 35 minutes, uncovered, until rolls are golden brown. To serve, spoon the syrup from pan over the dumplings.

BROWN SUGAR APPLE DUMPLINGS

Makes 4 servings

Pie Crust

2 cups all-purpose flour
1 teaspoon salt
$^1/_2$ cup shortening
2 tablespoons cold butter, cut into pieces
$^1/_3$–$^1/_2$ cup cold water, divided

Apples

2 large baking apples (such as Rome Beauty, Jonagold, or Pink Lady), cored and peeled*
4 tablespoons sugar
2 teaspoons cinnamon
1 tablespoon cold butter or margarine, divided

Syrup

$^3/_4$ cup firmly packed brown sugar
3 tablespoons butter or margarine
$^1/_4$ cup water
$^1/_4$ cup cream

Preheat oven to 425 degrees. For the crust, place flour, salt, shortening, and butter in a food processor; pulse until well mixed. Flour should begin to stick together when pinched between two fingers. With the cover on, add ¼ cup water through the feed tube; add more water, 1 tablespoon at a time, until a dough ball forms. *Continued >*

*You can leave the apples unpeeled, if you wish.

Remove dough and divide in half. On a floured surface, roll out the first half into a 14-inch square. Cut edges with a sharp knife to make a clean square; save scraps for patching.

To form the dumpling, move dough square to a baking dish large enough to hold 2 large dumplings side by side without touching. Place 1 apple in the center of the square. Mix sugar and cinnamon together and pour half into the cored hole, letting excess spill onto the outside of the apple. Add $\frac{1}{2}$ tablespoon butter to the core with the sugar. Wet the edges of the dough. Bring up the 4 corners of dough and fold over top of apple, pressing to seal all the way around. If there isn't enough dough to seal at the top, roll out a small piece from the scraps. Wet it on one side, lay the wet side over top of the apple, and press to seal it to the rest of the dough. Make a small vent hole in the crust at the top of the apple. Repeat process for second apple.

For the syrup, heat brown sugar, butter, and water in a small saucepan over medium heat until the sugar liquefies. Let simmer while it reduces and thickens a bit. Keep warm while apples bake.

Bake dumplings on center rack in the oven for about 50 minutes (check after 45 minutes), until crust turns golden brown. Ladle syrup over the dumplings 3 times, about every 15 minutes, during baking. Remove from oven and let cool for 5 minutes before moving to plates or bowls. Pour any remaining syrup and the cream into the baking dish to combine with the thickened syrup left in the dish. Spoon cream sauce over the dumplings.

WONTON APPLE POCKETS À LA MODE

Makes 4 servings

2 sweet-tart apples (such as Gala or Granny Smith), peeled and cored*
1 tablespoon butter or margarine
Vegetable oil, for frying
8 large egg roll wrappers
$1/4$ teaspoon cinnamon
2 tablespoons sugar
$1/4$ cup powdered sugar
Vanilla ice cream

Slice prepared apples into rings. In a large frying pan, melt butter and sauté apples over medium heat for about 3 minutes. Transfer apples to a plate. Rinse frying pan and wipe clean.

Pour vegetable oil into the frying pan about $1/4$ inch deep. Heat oil over medium heat until it begins to bubble around the edge, about 325 degrees.

Prepare the apple pockets by laying 4 egg roll wrappers on a flat surface. Wet the outside edges by running a paper towel dipped in water around the rims. Arrange 2–3 apple rings overlapping in the center of each wrapper (cut rings in half if they don't fit). Mix together the

cinnamon and sugar then sprinkle apples with the mixture. Top each wrapper with a second wrapper, and press edges together to create a seal. If your apple rings are small or thin, you can use only 1 egg roll wrapper and fold it like an envelope around the apple slices, as shown in the photos.

Using tongs, gently transfer 1 apple pocket into the oil, and let cook for about 30 seconds, until wrapper is blistered and golden. Turn pocket over and cook the other side for about 30 seconds. Transfer to paper towels to drain. Repeat with the other 3 apple pockets.

Lightly sprinkle pockets with powdered sugar and serve with a scoop of ice cream.

*An apple corer or melon baller can be used to remove the core without cutting the apple in half. If this seems inconvenient, halve the apples and slice half-rings.

NOTE: This recipe was inspired by my niece Stacy Ashmead.

RUSTIC APPLE TART

Makes 6 servings

1 (9-inch) unbaked pie crust
4 tart red apples
1 teaspoon freshly squeezed lemon juice
$^3/_4$ cup sugar
$^1/_4$ teaspoon cinnamon
$^1/_2$ teaspoon nutmeg
1 tablespoon cornstarch
$^1/_2$ teaspoon salt

Preheat oven to 400 degrees. Roll out pie crust to a 10-inch circle. Let rest for 1 minute then transfer to a baking sheet or pizza pan.

Core and thinly slice apples into a medium bowl, leaving the skin on. Toss with lemon juice. Mix the sugar, cinnamon, nutmeg, cornstarch, and salt in a small bowl; sprinkle over the apples. Toss and let sit for 5–10 minutes while the juice starts to come out of the apples.

Transfer apples with juice to the middle of the pie dough, being careful not to let the juice run off the edges. Working around the outside edges, carefully fold the dough up and over the apples, overlapping with each fold, being careful not to tear the dough, and leaving the center of the tart open.

Bake on the middle rack of the oven for about 40 minutes, until apples are tender.

BURNISHED-APPLE TART RING

Makes 6–8 servings

1 recipe Tart Dough (recipe follows)
³/4 cup sugar
2 teaspoons cinnamon
1 tablespoon cornstarch
6–8 tart apples, cored and peeled
Whipped cream, for serving

Prepare tart shell ahead and leave chilling in the refrigerator until ready to use.

Preheat oven to 425 degrees. Mix sugar, cinnamon, and cornstarch together in a small bowl and set aside.

Cut apples in half, and then cut each half into 6–8 slices. Arrange apple slices in overlapping rings in the tart shell to cover the dough, starting at the outside. Pile remaining apple slices in the middle. Sprinkle sugar mixture evenly over all the apples. Place tart pan on a baking sheet, cover loosely with foil, and bake for 20 minutes.

Reduce heat to 375 degrees and bake for 15 minutes; remove foil and bake for 10 minutes more. If apple edges are not tinged with brown, place tart under the broiler for 1–2 minutes, watching carefully. Let cool on a wire rack. Serve at room temperature with a dollop of whipped cream.

Tart Dough

Makes enough for 1 (10-inch) tart or 6 tartlets

1³/4 cups all-purpose flour
1/2 teaspoon salt
5 teaspoons sugar
1/4 cup shortening
2 tablespoons cream cheese, softened
2 tablespoons butter, room temperature
4 tablespoons ice water, divided

Place all ingredients except water in a food processor, and pulse until mixture looks like cornmeal. Add 3 tablespoons water and pulse just until mixture is moist and gathering, but not yet a ball. If mixture doesn't gather, add 1 more tablespoon of water. Carefully remove dough from processor bowl and gather into a ball (if too sticky to handle, dust ball with a little flour). Wrap in plastic and refrigerate for 30 minutes or overnight.

When ready to make the tart, place dough ball between two sheets of plastic wrap, and roll out to the shape of your tart pan plus 1–1 ½ inches for the sides. Fit dough into tart pan and press into the bottom and up the sides. Run the rolling pin along the top of the tart pan to cut dough off cleanly; remove excess dough. Chill while preparing filling. Bake according to tart recipe.

MAPLE RAISIN-APPLE TARTLETS

Makes 6 servings

1 recipe Tart Dough (page 85)
$^1/_3$ cup raisins, soaked in hot water for 10 minutes and drained
$1^1/_4$ cups peeled and chopped crisp, sweet apple
$^1/_3$ cup sugar
1 teaspoon cinnamon
2 teaspoons all-purpose flour
2 tablespoons maple syrup (preferably pure)

Preheat oven to 350 degrees.

Roll Tart Dough into a circle about 14 inches around and ⅛ inch thick. Cut 6 circles of dough using a wide-mouth bottle ring or cylinder. Mold dough into the cups of a 6-cup muffin tin, centering them carefully. Chill while preparing apple filling.

In a large bowl, stir together remaining ingredients and spoon carefully and evenly into the muffin cups. Place muffin tin on a baking sheet and bake for 17–20 minutes; test the crusts for doneness with a toothpick or metal skewer. Cool to room temperature and allow to set slightly before serving.

EASY APPLE STRUDEL

Makes 8–10 servings

1 (9-inch) pie crust, rolled thin to about 8 x 12 inches
3 cups roughly chopped cooking apples
2 teaspoons freshly squeezed lemon juice
$^1/_2$ cup raisins, softened
$^1/_4$ cup chopped pecans
$^1/_2$ cup sugar
2 tablespoons all-purpose flour
$^1/_4$ teaspoon nutmeg
$^1/_8$ teaspoon salt
Whipped cream, for serving

Preheat oven to 350 degrees. Line a baking sheet with parchment paper to prevent sticking. Place dough on parchment.

In a medium bowl, stir together apples, lemon juice, raisins, pecans, sugar, flour, nutmeg, and salt. Spoon filling onto a long side of the dough, about 3 inches from the edge and ends. Use the parchment paper to carefully fold dough over the filling, and roll the dough to completely encase the apples. Wet the outer edge of the crust with water before rolling it up. Seal the outer edge of dough by pressing lightly. Position the strudel in the center of the parchment and seal the ends. Bake for 35–40 minutes, until the crust begins to brown.

Remove from oven and allow to cool on the baking sheet. Slice and serve with whipped cream.

APPLE FRITTERS

Makes 12–15 fritters

1 box hot roll mix*
1 tablespoon butter or margarine
1 egg
1 cup hot water
3 apples
Canola oil, for frying
1 cup powdered sugar
$^1/_4$ cup water

In a large bowl, mix the roll mix with yeast (from the mix), butter, egg, and water according to package directions. Knead lightly in the bowl a few times. Cover and let rise for about 15 minutes.

Cut apples into 10 wedges then into pieces about $^1/_3$ inch long. Add apples to the dough and work them through with your hands. Cover and let rise for about 15 minutes in a warm spot.

Add about 1 $^1/_2$–2 inches of oil to a frying pan. Heat on medium high to about 350 degrees, until a small piece of dough and apple gently dropped into the oil browns quickly (about 1 minute). Transfer about $^1/_3$ cup of apple and dough mixture to the hot oil, being very careful not to splash. When adequately browned, turn fritters over with tongs to brown other side. Transfer cooked fritters to paper towels to drain.

Mix powdered sugar and water in a medium bowl to make a glaze. Dip warm or cool fritters into the sugar mixture to coat. Let drip on a wire rack. Serve warm or cool.

*Usually found near the cornbread and cake mixes.

Cakes, Cobblers, Breads & Sweet Treats

APPLE UPSIDE-DOWN SPICE CAKE

Makes 10–12 servings

2 tablespoons brown sugar
$^1/_3$ cup slivered almonds
3 large tart apples, divided: 1 $^1/_2$ apples thinly sliced*; 1 $^1/_2$ apples grated
1$^1/_2$ cups spice cake mix
3 tablespoons canola oil
2 eggs
2 tablespoons apple juice
2 tablespoons butter
Whipped cream, optional

Preheat oven to 350 degrees. Line a 9-inch round cake pan with parchment or waxed paper. Sprinkle brown sugar over the parchment and ring the circumference with almonds. Arrange half of the apple slices like flower petals in the center of the cake pan.

In a large bowl, mix the grated apple, cake mix, oil, eggs, and apple juice until thoroughly blended. Spread the batter evenly over bottom of cake pan. Bake for 30 minutes, or until a toothpick inserted into the center comes out clean. Cool for 10 minutes before inverting onto a plate. Carefully remove the parchment paper and discard.

For decorating the cake, sauté the remaining apple slices in butter over medium heat until they soften a bit. Arrange sautéed slices in a an overlapping circle. Roll the reserved long apple peel tightly to resemble a rose; set it in the middle.

Serve plain or with a dollop of whipped cream.

*Peel the apple in a manner that keeps the entire peel in a long piece, to be rolled into a rose for decoration.

GRANDMA'S APPLE CAKE

Makes 12–16 servings

2 cups sugar
2 eggs
¹/₂ cup canola oil
2 teaspoons vanilla extract
4 cups grated apples
2 cups all-purpose flour
2 teaspoons baking soda
¹/₂ teaspoon salt
2 teaspoons cinnamon
1 cup chopped nuts (such as pecans, walnuts, or almonds), optional
1 (16-ounce) container cream cheese frosting

Preheat oven to 350 degrees. Oil and flour a 9 x 13-inch baking pan.

Combine sugar, eggs, oil, and vanilla in a large bowl using an electric mixer. Beat for 2 minutes to lighten batter. Add apples and mix on medium speed until incorporated. In a separate bowl, mix together flour, baking soda, salt, and cinnamon. Add dry ingredients to wet ingredients and mix until well combined. Stir in the nuts.

Pour batter into prepared pan and spread evenly. Bake for 45 minutes, or until a toothpick inserted into the middle comes out clean. Remove from oven and let cool in pan on a wire rack. Frost with cream cheese frosting.

APPLE BREAD PUDDING WITH CARAMEL SAUCE

Makes 8–10 servings

4–5 cups bread cubes made from day-old artisan bread
4 tart apples, peeled and chopped
$^{1}/_{3}$ cup raisins
1 teaspoon cinnamon
1 teaspoon salt
3 cups milk
6 tablespoons butter or margarine
$^{1}/_{2}$–$^{3}/_{4}$ cup firmly packed brown sugar
1 teaspoon vanilla extract
3 eggs, beaten
Heavy cream
Caramel sundae syrup

Preheat oven to 350 degrees. Spray a 3- to 4-quart casserole dish with cooking oil. Heat enough water for a water bath.

Place bread, apples, and raisins in prepared dish. Sprinkle with cinnamon and salt. In a medium saucepan, heat milk and butter over medium-high heat until steam begins to rise. Remove from heat and stir in brown sugar and vanilla until sugar dissolves. Temper eggs by stirring in about ¼ cup hot milk, a little at a time, then stir the eggs into the milk. Ladle milk mixture evenly over bread and apples to moisten bread.

Set casserole dish inside a larger baking pan that can serve as a water bath. Place baking pan in oven and carefully pour hot water into the outer pan until it reaches about 1 ½ inches up the side of casserole dish. Bake for 1 hour, or until custard is set and top of bread is light brown. Serve with a drizzle of cream and caramel syrup.

ALMOND APPLE CHEESECAKE

Makes 12 servings

Crust

2 cups crushed almond windmill cookies
$1/2$ cup all-purpose flour
$1/4$ cup sugar
$1/2$ cup (1 stick) butter or margarine, melted

Filling

2 (8-ounce) packages cream cheese, room temperature
$1/2$ cup firmly packed brown sugar
1 teaspoon almond extract
2 eggs
2 tablespoons sour cream
2 large or 3 medium tart apples, peeled and sliced
$1/3$ cup sliced almonds
Whipped cream

Preheat oven to 350 degrees. Stir the cookie crumbs, flour, and sugar together in a large bowl. Add the butter and mix until all crumbs are moistened. Press mixture into the bottom of a 9-inch springform pan and bake for 10 minutes. Let cool for about 15 minutes.

Increase oven heat to 400 degrees.

Beat the cream cheese, brown sugar, and almond extract together until light and airy. Add eggs and sour cream and mix well. Spread filling evenly inside crust. Arrange apple slices in circles on top of the filling and sprinkle with almonds. Bake for 20 minutes. Reduce heat to 350 degrees and bake for 40 minutes more, or until a skewer inserted into the center comes out clean. Remove from oven and let cool. Refrigerate for 3 hours, or overnight. Serve chilled with a dollop of whipped cream.

APPLE SPICE CUPCAKES

Makes 18 servings

1 cup sugar
$^1/_4$ cup shortening
1 egg
$^1/_2$ teaspoon salt
1 teaspoon cinnamon
$^1/_2$ teaspoon ginger
$^1/_2$ teaspoon ground cloves
$^1/_2$ teaspoon ground allspice
1 teaspoon vanilla extract
2 medium Golden Delicious apples, halved, cored, and grated
2$^1/_2$ cups flour
2 teaspoons baking powder
$^1/_2$ teaspoon baking soda
1 tablespoon vinegar
1 cup milk
1 (16-ounce) container vanilla frosting

Preheat oven to 375 degrees. Prepare muffin tins with cupcake papers or spray oil. In a large bowl, beat first 4 ingredients together on high until light and airy, about 1 ½ minutes. Add cinnamon, ginger, cloves, allspice, vanilla, and apples; mix well.

In a medium bowl, add flour, baking powder, and baking soda; mix well to combine. In a separate bowl, stir the vinegar into the milk. Add the milk and flour mixtures to the apple mixture alternately, stirring after each addition, until well incorporated. Mix on high for about 2 minutes, until batter is light and airy.

Fill each muffin cup about ⅔ full. Bake for 18–20 minutes, until cakes begin to turn golden and a toothpick inserted into the center comes out clean, Remove cupcakes to a cooling rack. Frost with vanilla frosting when completely cool.

MELT-IN-YOUR-MOUTH APPLE BUNDT CAKE

Makes 10–12 servings

1 (15.25-ounce) package Betty Crocker Super Moist Golden Vanilla cake mix
2 tablespoons all-purpose flour
3 eggs
$^1/_2$ cup vegetable oil
1 cup water
5–6 medium cooking apples, cored, peeled, and sliced
3 tablespoons brown sugar
$^1/_2$ cup plus 2 tablespoons sugar
Whipped cream
Caramel sundae syrup

Preheat oven to 350 degrees. Oil and flour a Bundt pan; tap out excess flour.

Stir cake mix and flour together in a large bowl. Add eggs, oil, and water; mix well. Pour a little more than half of the batter into the bottom of the Bundt pan; distribute evenly. Place apple slices on top of batter, all around the ring. Combine the brown sugar and the sugar, and sprinkle about ¾ of the combined sugars over the apples. Spoon remaining batter evenly over apples and sprinkle with remaining sugar.

Bake for 38–42 minutes, until a skewer inserted from the side to the center comes out clean and cake is just beginning to pull away from sides of pan. Remove from oven and cool on a wire rack until pan is cool enough to handle. Use a narrow rubber spatula to gently loosen cake from sides of pan. Place a cake plate over top of pan and invert to release cake onto the plate. Serve with whipped cream and caramel syrup.

STOVETOP CRAN-APPLE COBBLER

Makes 6-8 servings

Filling

4 large or 6 medium cooking apples, cored and peeled
1 tablespoon cornstarch mixed with 1 tablespoon water
1 tablespoon brown sugar
$^{1}/_{4}$ teaspoon salt
$^{1}/_{4}$ teaspoon nutmeg or mace
1 teaspoon freshly squeezed lemon juice
1 cup cranberry juice

Dumplings

1 cup biscuit mix
2 tablespoons sugar
$^{3}/_{4}$ cup cranberry juice
$^{1}/_{4}$ teaspoon nutmeg

Cut apples into large chunks and place in a large frying pan (preferably cast iron). Whisk cornstarch mixture, brown sugar, salt, nutmeg, lemon juice, and cranberry juice together in a small bowl until solids have dissolved. Pour juice mixture evenly over apples.

In a medium bowl, combine biscuit mix, sugar, and cranberry juice just until moistened. Dot rounded teaspoonfuls of batter over the apples until all the batter has been used, and then sprinkle with nutmeg. Cover pan tightly with foil or a lid and cook over medium high until liquid begins to boil. Reduce heat and let simmer for 20 minutes, until a toothpick inserted into a center biscuit comes out clean. Remove cover and continue cooking for 5 minutes to brown. Serve warm.

OLD-TIMEY APPLE PUDDING WITH NUTMEG CREAM SAUCE

Makes 10–12 servings

Pudding

2 cups firmly packed brown sugar
$^1/_2$ cup (1 stick) butter or margarine, room temperature
2 eggs
2 teaspoons vanilla extract
4 cups grated unpeeled apple
1 cup soft raisins
2 cups all-purpose flour
2 teaspoons baking soda
$^1/_2$ teaspoon salt
$^1/_2$ teaspoon cinnamon
$^1/_2$ teaspoon nutmeg
1 cup slivered almonds, optional

Nutmeg Cream Sauce

1 cup sugar
$^1/_4$ cup ($^1/_2$ stick) butter or margarine
1 cup cream, whipping or heavy
$^1/_4$ cup half-and-half
2 teaspoons cornstarch mixed with 2 teaspoons water
2 teaspoons vanilla extract
$^1/_2$ teaspoon nutmeg

Preheat oven to 325 degrees. Spray a heavy, covered casserole dish or 10- to 12-inch Dutch oven with cooking oil and dust with flour. Tap out excess flour.

In a large bowl, cream the sugar and butter together. Add eggs and vanilla and mix until batter is light and airy, about 2 ½ minutes. Mix in apples and raisins on medium speed until incorporated. In a separate bowl, combine flour, baking soda, salt, cinnamon, nutmeg, and almonds. Add dry ingredients to wet ingredients and fold together until well combined. Pour batter into prepared dish and spread evenly. Cover and bake for 60–75 minutes, or until a toothpick inserted into the center comes out clean. Remove from oven and let cool on a wire rack. Serve with warm Nutmeg Cream Sauce.

For the sauce, heat sugar, butter, cream, and half-and-half in a small saucepan over medium heat, stirring frequently, until sugar is dissolved. Add cornstarch mixture and bring just to a boil. Remove from heat and stir in vanilla and nutmeg.

APPLE PANDOWDY

Makes 8–10 servings

4–5 cups roughly chopped peeled apples
$1/4$ cup freshly squeezed lemon juice
$1/2$ cup (1 stick) butter or margarine
1 cup apple juice
$3/4$ cup sugar
2 teaspoons cinnamon
1 tablespoon cornstarch

Dumplings

$1^1/3$ cups biscuit mix
$1/2$ cup milk
$1/3$ cup sugar
$1/2$ teaspoon cinnamon

Preheat oven to 375 degrees. Place apples in a large bowl and toss with lemon juice.

Melt butter in a large ovenproof frying pan. Sauté apples for 3–4 minutes then add apple juice. Combine sugar, cinnamon, and cornstarch; sprinkle evenly over apples. Heat over medium-high heat until liquid begins to bubble.

For the dumplings, mix biscuit mix and milk together in a separate bowl. When apples are hot and liquid is lightly bubbling, drop batter by the tablespoonful onto the apples until all has been used. Stir sugar and cinnamon together and sprinkle over the batter. Place frying pan into the oven and cook for 20–25 minutes, until biscuit top is lightly golden and a toothpick inserted into the center comes out clean.

PUMPKIN-APPLE MUFFINS

Makes 1 dozen muffins

1 egg, beaten
1 cup pumpkin purée
2 teaspoons molasses, optional
$^3/_4$ cup sugar
$^1/_2$ teaspoon pumpkin pie spice
$^3/_4$ cup evaporated milk
2 cups chopped peeled apple (wrinkled apples are best, as they cook faster)
2 scant cups all-purpose flour (1–2 tablespoons less than full cups)
$2^1/_2$ teaspoons baking powder
1 teaspoon salt

Preheat oven to 400 degrees. Spray a muffin tin with cooking oil.

In a large bowl, whisk together the egg, pumpkin, molasses, sugar, and pie spice. Stir in milk. Fold in apples. In a separate bowl, combine flour, baking powder, and salt. Add flour to pumpkin mixture and mix well.

Fill each muffin cup $^2/_3$ full with batter. Bake for 20 minutes, or until lightly browned on top and a toothpick inserted into the center comes out clean. Turn muffins out onto cooling rack.

APPLE 'N' CHEESE DROP BISCUITS

Makes about 1 dozen biscuits

1 cup whole-wheat flour
1 cup all-purpose flour
1 tablespoon baking powder
$^1/_2$ teaspoon baking soda
1 teaspoon salt
$^1/_8$ teaspoon thyme leaves or ground sage
$^1/_3$ cup shortening
$^3/_4$ cup grated cheddar cheese
2 apples, grated
$^3/_4$ cup plus 2 tablespoons milk

Preheat oven to 425 degrees.

In a medium bowl, stir together the flours, baking powder, baking soda, salt, and thyme. Cut in shortening with a pastry blender or 2 knives. Mix cheese and apples into the flour. Pour in $^3/_4$ cup milk and mix until all the flour is moistened; do not overmix. If needed, add remaining milk, 1 tablespoon at a time, to gather flour from sides of the bowl into the dough.

Drop dough by spoonfuls onto an ungreased baking sheet. Bake for 12–15 minutes, until tops brown lightly and centers are cooked.

BUTTERSCOTCH APPLE MUFFINS

Makes 12–15 muffins

$1^1/_2$ cups plus 2 tablespoons all-purpose flour
2 packets instant apple cinnamon oatmeal
1 teaspoon baking power
1 teaspoon baking soda
$^1/_4$ teaspoon salt
$^1/_4$ cup brown sugar
$^1/_4$ teaspoon cinnamon
$^1/_8$ teaspoon nutmeg
2 eggs, lightly beaten
$^3/_4$ cup milk
2 apples, grated
$^3/_4$ cup butterscotch chips

Preheat oven to 375 degrees. Spray muffin tin with cooking oil.

In a medium bowl, combine flour, oatmeal, baking powder, baking soda, salt, sugar, cinnamon, and nutmeg. Add eggs, milk, apples, and butterscotch chips and fold together until dry ingredients are well moistened. Spoon batter into cups to nearly full.

Bake for 15–20 minutes, or until lightly browned on top and a toothpick inserted into the center comes out clean. Turn out onto cooling rack.

FOOD PROCESSOR APPLE BREAD

Makes 2 medium loaves

4 medium apples, cored, halved, and quartered
$^1/_4$ cup walnuts or pecans
$^1/_2$ cup rolled oats
$^1/_2$ cup plus 2 tablespoons butter or margarine, room temperature
1 cup firmly packed brown sugar
2 cups all-purpose flour
1 teaspoon baking powder
1 teaspoon baking soda
1 teaspoon cinnamon
$^1/_2$ teaspoon salt
1 egg
$^3/_4$ cup evaporated milk

Preheat oven to 375 degrees. Spray two 8-inch loaf pans with cooking oil, and then line with waxed paper to fit the bottom and extend up both ends with a little overhang for handles.

Place apples, walnuts, oats, butter, and brown sugar in a food processor. Pulse 10–12 times, until apples are finely chopped. Scrape down sides of processor bowl. Add flour, baking powder, baking soda, cinnamon, salt, egg, and milk; process until combined. Divide batter between the loaf pans.

Place pans on a baking sheet and bake for 35–40 minutes, turning sheet halfway through cooking time to ensure even baking. When bread is pulling away from sides of pan and a skewer inserted into the center of a loaf comes out clean, it is done. Cool in pans on a wire rack for 10 minutes, then lift loaves from pans, remove paper, and let cool completely before slicing.

APPLE BROWN BETTY

Makes 8–10 servings

8 cups chopped apples, several varieties mixed
1 cup sugar, divided
1 teaspoon nutmeg, plus more for garnish
$^3/_4$ loaf whole-wheat bread (to make about 5 cups crumbs)
1$^1/_2$ teaspoons cinnamon
$^1/_2$ cup (1 stick) butter or margarine, melted
$^1/_2$ pint whipping cream
1 tablespoon confectioners' sugar
$^1/_2$ teaspoon vanilla extract

Preheat oven to 400 degrees. Spray a 9 x 13-inch baking dish with cooking oil.

Toss apples with $^3/_4$ cup sugar and 1 teaspoon nutmeg in a large bowl.

In a food processor, process bread to crumbs with remaining sugar and the cinnamon. Add butter and continue processing until all crumbs are moistened. Place a layer of bread crumbs in the baking dish. Spread apples over crumbs and then top with more bread crumbs.

Cover loosely with foil and bake for 25 minutes. Reduce oven to 350 degrees and continue baking for 20 minutes. During the last 5–10 minutes, remove foil to brown top. Meanwhile, whip the cream with confectioners' sugar and vanilla until soft peaks form.

Remove the betty from the oven and serve with whipped cream. Sprinkle very lightly with nutmeg.

APPLE DUTCH BABY

Makes 2–4 servings

3 tablespoons sugar
2 teaspoons cinnamon
2 large Golden Delicious apples
4 tablespoons butter
3 eggs
$1/2$ teaspoon salt
$1/2$ teaspoon vanilla extract
$1/2$ cup milk
$1/2$ cup all-purpose flour
Pure maple syrup

Preheat oven to 425 degrees. Mix sugar and cinnamon together and set aside.

Peel, core, and slice apples into wedges; cut wedges into fourths.

Melt butter in a 10- or 12-inch cast iron or other ovenproof skillet over medium heat. Add apple pieces, sprinkle with cinnamon sugar, and sauté for about 7 minutes, until apples just begin to soften. Stir a couple of times while cooking.

In a medium bowl, whisk together eggs, salt, vanilla, and milk. Sprinkle flour over eggs and whisk together until lumps are gone. Pour batter over apples and tilt pan to distribute batter evenly. Bake for 15–20 minutes, until the pancake batter is puffed up and cooked through. Remove from oven, loosen the pancake from the skillet, and invert it onto a serving platter. Cut into wedges and serve with maple syrup.

BLUEBERRY-APPLE BIRD'S NEST

Makes 8-12 servings

1 loaf frozen bread dough, thawed
$^1/_2$ cup (1 stick) butter or margarine, room temperature
3 cups chopped apples
$^3/_4$ cup fresh blueberries
$^1/_2$ teaspoon cinnamon
$^1/_2$ cup sugar
Butter or vanilla glaze

Spray an 8-inch round cake pan with deep sides or a round casserole dish with cooking oil.

Roll dough into a 10–12-inch circle. Mold dough to the baking dish and brush lightly with most of the butter. Fill center of dough with apples and blueberries then sprinkle with cinnamon and sugar. Fold dough toward center of the "nest," but do not completely cover fruit (dough can be uneven). Brush exposed top surface of dough with remaining butter. Let rise for 20 minutes.

Meanwhile, preheat oven to 375 degrees. Bake for 30–40 minutes, until lightly browned on top and cooked through (test by inserting a skewer into center of dough; if it goes in without resistance, bread is cooked). You may cover bread lightly with foil when it begins to brown to prevent overbrowning. Reduce oven to 350 degrees if the bottom of crust is getting too brown. Remove from oven and let cool on a wire rack for about 10 minutes before removing from dish. Serve with butter or vanilla glaze.

APPLE CRISP

3 pounds (about 8–10) tart apples, cored and thinly sliced
1 tablespoon freshly squeezed lemon juice
$2/3$ cup granulated Splenda or Truvia
2 teaspoons cinnamon
$1/4$ teaspoon nutmeg
$1/4$ teaspoons ginger
8 square graham crackers
4 gingersnap cookies
$1/2$ cup ground nuts (walnuts, pecans, almonds)
$1/2$ cup (1 stick) butter or margarine, melted
Whipped cream

Preheat oven to 350 degrees. Spray an 8 x 10-inch baking dish with cooking oil.

Cut apple slices in half and arrange in baking dish. Sprinkle lemon juice over apples.

In a medium bowl, mix together Splenda, cinnamon, nutmeg, and ginger. Sprinkle evenly over apples.

In a food processor, process crackers and cookies to a fine crumb. Transfer crumbs to a bowl and stir in nuts. Pour ⅓ of the butter over crumb mixture and mix to moisten. Pour another ⅓ of the butter into the crumbs and mix well. If crumbs are sufficiently moistened (they don't have to stick together), drizzle remaining butter over the apples.

Distribute crumbs loosely over the apples. Bake for 45–50 minutes, until apples are cooked and crumbs begin to brown. Serve warm with whipped cream.

APPLESAUCE CHOCOLATE CHIP COOKIES

Makes 4 dozen (2-inch) cookies

1 cup sugar
$^{1}/_{4}$ cup canola oil
1 egg
1 $^{1}/_{2}$ cups applesauce
2 $^{1}/_{2}$ cups all-purpose flour
1 teaspoon baking soda
$^{1}/_{2}$ teaspoon salt
1 teaspoon cinnamon
$^{1}/_{4}$ teaspoon ground cloves
1 cup semisweet chocolate chips
$^{1}/_{2}$ cup finely chopped pecans

Preheat oven to 350 degrees. Spray a baking sheet with cooking oil.

Place sugar, oil, egg, and applesauce in a medium bowl; stir together. In a large bowl, combine flour, baking soda, salt, cinnamon and cloves; add to the applesauce mixture and combine. Stir in chocolate chips and pecans. Dough will be the consistency of a thick cake batter.

Drop generously rounded teaspoonfuls about 3 inches apart on prepared baking sheet. Bake cookies in batches for 15 minutes. This cookie has a cake-like texture.

NOTE: This dough freezes well. Allow to thaw in the refrigerator before baking.

STOVETOP BAKED APPLES

Makes 4 servings

4 Golden Delicious apples
$1/2$ cup sugar
$1^1/2$ teaspoons cinnamon
2 teaspoons butter or margarine, divided
Sweetened whipped cream

Using a melon baller, remove cores from apples starting at the stem end. Do not remove the blossom end of the apples. In a small bowl, mix sugar and cinnamon together. Set apples upright in a wide pan or frying pan with a lid. Drop ½ teaspoon butter into each apple then fill the holes with cinnamon sugar.

Pour about 1 inch of water into the pan. Cover pan and cook for 40 minutes, or until apples are soft; test with a knife after 35 minutes. Serve hot in bowls with a generous portion of whipped cream.

RHUBARB-APPLE CONSERVE

Makes about 3 pints

3 cups sliced rhubarb
3 cups chopped tart apple
3 cups sugar
$^1/_4$ cup water
$^3/_4$ cup golden raisins
$^1/_2$ cup coarsely chopped pecans or walnuts
1 (1.75-ounce) package powdered pectin

Place all ingredients except pectin in a large saucepan and bring to a boil, stirring frequently. Reduce heat and simmer, covered, for about 40 minutes, stirring frequently, until apple is soft and begins to turn translucent. Stir in pectin and bring to a light boil; continue stirring for 5 minutes.

Carefully ladle conserve into clean jars using a wide-mouth funnel, and cover tightly with lids. Let set until jars are cool to the touch, or overnight (or process in a hot water bath for shelf storage).

Use within 2 days, or refrigerate for up to 6 weeks. Even though jars may seal on their own, they will not be safe for long-term shelf storage unless they have been processed in a hot water bath.

SLOW-COOKER APPLE BUTTER

Makes about 2 cups

4 cups peeled and roughly chopped apples
1 cup sugar
1 teaspoon cinnamon
$^1/_2$ teaspoon nutmeg
$^1/_4$ teaspoon ground cloves
$^1/_2$ cup apple cider

Place all ingredients in a slow cooker and stir. Cover and cook on high for 1 hour. Continue cooking on low overnight, or up to 10 hours. Purée with an immersion blender until smooth (or let cool slightly and transfer to a food processor or blender for puréeing). Keeps well in refrigerator, tightly covered, for up to 6 weeks.

CHUNKY CINNAMON APPLESAUCE

Makes about 1 quart

5–6 large Golden Delicious apples
2 tablespoons sugar, or to taste
1 teaspoon cinnamon

Peel, core, and quarter apples. Place in a large heavy-bottom saucepan with about ⅓ cup water, just enough to prevent apples from sticking until they begin to release their own juices. Cover pan with a lid and cook over medium heat until apples are soft, about 30 minutes, stirring frequently to prevent sticking.

Use a potato masher to mash the apples in the pan, or transfer to a food processor bowl and pulse a couple of times before returning to the pan.

Combine sugar with cinnamon and stir into the apples. Continue cooking until sugar dissolves. Let applesauce cool then transfer to a jar or plastic container for storing in the refrigerator. Keeps in refrigerator for about 10 days.

Index

Acorn Squash, Apple-Stuffed, 66
acorn squash, in Savory Sausage-and-
    Apple Rice Stuffing, 58
almonds:
    Almond Apple Cheesecake, 97
    Apple Upside-Down Spice Cake, 92
    Company Pilaf, 70
    Old-Timey Apple Pudding with
        Nutmeg Cream Sauce, 102
    Snappy Apple Salad, 11
Apple Bread Pudding with Caramel
    Sauce, 95
Apple Brown Betty, 111
Apple Butter, Slow-Cooker, 123
Apple Cider Pot Roast, Slow-Cooker, 42
Apple Crisp, 117
Apple Dutch Baby, 113
Apple Fritters, 90
apple jelly, in Turkey Meatballs with
    Apple-Dijon Glaze, 47
apple juice:
    Apple Pandowdy, 104
    Beet and Apple Soup, 28
    Butternut-Apple Soup, 29
    Pumpkin-Apple Soup with Bacon, 26
    Savory Sausage-and-Apple Rice
        Stuffing, 58
    Sweet Potato, Orange, and Apple
        Bake, 52
Apple 'N' Cheese Drop Biscuits, 107
Apple Pandowdy, 104
Apple Slaw, 24
Apple Spice Cupcakes, 98
Apple Upside-Down Spice Cake, 92
Apple-Link Salad, 15
Apple-Stuffed Acorn Squash, 66
Apple-Stuffed Chicken Breasts, 44
apples:
    Gala, in Curry Chicken Salad, 19
    Golden Delicious:
        Apple Dutch Baby, 113
        Apple Spice Cupcakes, 98
        Chunky Cinnamon Applesauce, 124
        Sausage and Apple Pasta, 59
        Stovetop Baked Apples, 120
    Granny Smith or green:
        Beet-Apple Salad, 14

Potato-Apple Gratin with Ham, 64
Snappy Apple Salad, 11
Stir-Fried Vegetables with Hoisin, 61
of choice:
    Almond Apple Cheesecake, 97
    Apple 'N' Cheese Drop Biscuits, 107
    Apple Bread Pudding with
        Caramel Sauce, 95
    Apple Brown Betty, 111
    Apple Crisp, 117
    Apple Fritters, 90
    Apple Pandowdy, 104
    Apple Upside-Down Spice
        Cake, 92
    Apple-Link Salad, 15
    Apple-Stuffed Acorn Squash, 66
    Apple-Stuffed Chicken Breasts, 44
    Baked Beans with Apple, 65
    Beet and Apple Soup, 28
    Blueberry-Apple Bird's Nest, 114
    Brown Sugar Apple Dumplings, 77
    Burnished-Apple Tart Ring, 84
    Butterscotch Apple Muffins, 108
    Cabbage and Apple Soup, 36
    Chicken Quesadillas with
        Apples & Brie, 23
    Cinnamon Crumble Apple Pie, 72
    Classic Double-Crust Apple
        Pie, 74
    Company Pilaf, 70
    Creamy Parsnip and Apple
        Soup, 33
    Curried Carrot-Apple Bisque, 32
    Dressed-Up Pork Medallions, 39
    Easy Apple Strudel, 89
    Food Processor Apple Bread, 110
    Full-Meal Oven Roast, 40
    Grandma's Apple Cake, 94
    Grilled Chicken, Apple, and
        Leek Salad, 13
    Maple Raisin-Apple Tartlets, 86
    Melt-In-Your-Mouth Apple
        Bundt Cake, 99
    Mini Apple Dumplings with
        Ginger Ale, 75
    Mini Turkey Meatloaves, 48
    O. J. Fruit Salad, 18

Old-Timey Apple Pudding with
    Nutmeg Cream Sauce, 102
Overnight Breakfast Casserole, 62
Parmesan Roasted Apple-
    Vegetable Medley, 56
Pimento Cream Soup, 34
Pistachio, Chicken, and Apple
    Salad, 12
Pork Chops with Sautéed
    Apples, 43
Pumpkin-Apple Muffins, 105
Pumpkin-Apple Soup with
    Bacon, 26
Red Lentil Soup with Sweet
    Potato and Apple, 31
Rhubarb-Apple Conserve, 121
Savory Sausage-and-Apple
    Rice Stuffing, 58
Slow-Cooker Apple Butter, 123
Slow-Cooker Apple Cider Pot
    Roast, 42
Spinach-Apple Sauté, 55
Stovetop Cran-Apple Cobbler, 100
Sunday Dutch Oven Pork, 41
Sweet Potato, Orange, and
    Apple Bake, 52
Sweet-and-Sour Cabbage and
    Apple Skillet, 50
Turkey Meatballs with Apple-
    Dijon Glaze, 47
Vegetable and Apple Curry, 54
Warm Five-Spice Apple Slaw, 53
Wonton Apple Pockets À La
    Mode, 80
red:
    Apple Slaw, 24
    Autumn Chicken Salad, 20
    Fruity Stuffing, 69
    Potato Salad with Bacon and
        Apples, 16
    Rustic Apple Tart, 83
Applesauce Chocolate Chip Cookies,
    118
Applesauce, Chunky Cinnamon, 124
Autumn Chicken Salad, 20
bacon:
    Baked Beans with Apple, 65

Potato Salad with Bacon and
   Apples, 16
Pumpkin-Apple Soup with Bacon, 26
Baked Apples, Stovetop, 120
Baked Beans with Apple, 65
banana, in O. J. Fruit Salad, 18
beef:
   ground, in Cabbage and Apple
      Soup, 36
   roast:
      Full-Meal Oven Roast, 40
      Slow-Cooker Apple Cider Pot
         Roast, 42
Beet and Apple Soup, 28
Beet-Apple Salad, 14
Betty, Apple Brown, 111
Bird's Nest, Blueberry-Apple, 114
Biscuits, Apple 'N' Cheese Drop, 107
Bisque, Curried Carrot-Apple, 32
Blueberry-Apple Bird's Nest, 114
Bread Pudding with Caramel Sauce,
   Apple, 95
Bread, Food Processor Apple, 110
Breakfast Casserole, Overnight, 62
Brie, Chicken Quesadillas with Apples &, 23
Brown Betty, Apple, 111
Brown Sugar Apple Dumplings, 77
Brussels sprouts:
   Full-Meal Oven Roast, 40
   Parmesan Roasted Apple-Vegetable
      Medley, 56
   Stir-Fried Vegetables with Hoisin, 61
Bundt Cake, Melt-In-Your-Mouth Apple, 99
Burnished-Apple Tart Ring, 84
butternut squash, in Parmesan Roasted
   Apple-Vegetable Medley, 56
Butternut-Apple Soup, 29
Butterscotch Apple Muffins, 108
cabbage:
   Apple Slaw, 24
   Cabbage and Apple Soup, 36
   Sweet-and-Sour Cabbage and
      Apple Skillet, 50
   Warm Five-Spice Apple Slaw, 53
cake:
   Apple Spice Cupcakes, 98
   Apple Upside-Down Spice Cake, 92
   Grandma's Apple Cake, 94
   Melt-In-Your-Mouth Apple Bundt Cake, 99
Carrot-Apple Bisque, Curried, 32

Casserole, Overnight Breakfast, 62
Cheese Drop Biscuits, Apple 'N,' 107
Cheesecake, Almond Apple, 97
chicken:
   Apple-Stuffed Chicken Breasts, 44
   Autumn Chicken Salad, 20
   Chicken Quesadillas with Apples &
      Brie, 23
   Curry Chicken Salad, 19
   Grilled Chicken, Apple, and Leek
      Salad, 13
   Pistachio, Chicken, and Apple Salad, 12
Chocolate Chip Cookies, Applesauce, 118
Cinnamon Applesauce, Chunky, 124
Cinnamon Crumble Apple Pie, 72
Cinnamon Crumble Topping, 72
Classic Double-Crust Apple Pie, 74
Cobbler, Stovetop Cran-Apple, 100
Company Pilaf, 70
Conserve, Rhubarb-Apple, 121
Cookies, Applesauce Chocolate Chip, 118
craisins, in Fruity Stuffing, 69
Cran-Apple Cobbler, Stovetop, 100
Creamy Parsnip and Apple Soup, 33
Crisp, Apple, 117
Cupcakes, Apple Spice, 98
Curried Carrot-Apple Bisque, 32
Curry Chicken Salad, 19
Curry, Vegetable and Apple, 54
Dressed-Up Pork Medallions, 39
Drop Biscuits, Apple 'N' Cheese, 107
Dumplings with Ginger Ale, Mini Apple, 75
Dumplings, Brown Sugar Apple, 77
Dutch Baby, Apple, 113
Dutch Oven Pork, Sunday, 41
Easy Apple Strudel, 89
fennel, in Parmesan Roasted Apple-
   Vegetable Medley, 56
Five-Spice Apple Slaw, Warm, 53
Food Processor Apple Bread, 110
Fritters, Apple, 90
Fruit Salad, O. J., 18
Fruity Stuffing, 69
Full-Meal Oven Roast, 40
garbanzo beans (chickpeas), in Beet-
   Apple Salad, 14
Ginger Ale, Mini Apple Dumplings with, 75
Grandma's Apple Cake, 94
grapes:
   Autumn Chicken Salad, 20

Curry Chicken Salad, 19
Gratin with Ham, Potato-Apple, 64
Grilled Chicken, Apple, and Leek Salad, 13
Ham, Potato-Apple Gratin with, 64
Hoisin, Stir-Fried Vegetables with, 61
Honey Mustard Vinaigrette, 16
Honey Vinaigrette, 13
kale, in Apple-Stuffed Chicken Breasts, 44
Kraft Pimento Cheese Spread, in
   Pimento Cream Soup, 34
leek:
   Chicken Quesadillas with Apples &
      Brie, 23
   Company Pilaf, 70
   Grilled Chicken, Apple, and Leek
      Salad, 13
   Sausage and Apple Pasta, 59
lettuce/salad greens:
   Autumn Chicken Salad, 20
   Beet-Apple Salad, 14
   Curry Chicken Salad, 19
   Pistachio, Chicken, and Apple Salad, 12
   Snappy Apple Salad, 11
Maple Raisin-Apple Tartlets, 86
Meatballs with Apple-Dijon Glaze,
   Turkey, 47
Meatloaves, Mini Turkey, 48
Melt-In-Your-Mouth Apple Bundt Cake, 99
Mini Apple Dumplings with Ginger Ale, 75
Muffins, Butterscotch Apple, 108
Muffins, Pumpkin-Apple, 105
mushrooms, in Dressed-Up Pork
   Medallions, 39
Nutmeg Cream Sauce, 102
O. J. Fruit Salad, 18
Old-Timey Apple Pudding with Nutmeg
   Cream Sauce, 102
orange, in O. J. Fruit Salad, 18
orange juice:
   O. J. Fruit Salad, 18
   Sweet Potato, Orange, and Apple
      Bake, 52
Overnight Breakfast Casserole, 62
Pandowdy, Apple, 104
   Parmesan Roasted Apple-Vegetable
      Medley, 56
parsnip:
   Creamy Parsnip and Apple Soup, 33
   Parmesan Roasted Apple-Vegetable
      Medley, 56

Pasta, Sausage and Apple, 59
peas:
    Snappy Apple Salad, 11
    Vegetable and Apple Curry, 54
pecans:
    Applesauce Chocolate Chip Cookies, 118
    Autumn Chicken Salad, 20
    Easy Apple Strudel, 89
    Rhubarb-Apple Conserve, 121
    Sweet Potato, Orange, and Apple
        Bake, 52
Pie Crust, 77
Pie, Cinnamon Crumble Apple, 72
Pie, Classic Double-Crust Apple, 74
Pilaf, Company, 70
Pimento Cream Soup, 34
pine nuts, in Spinach-Apple Sauté, 55
pineapple, in O. J. Fruit Salad, 18
Pistachio, Chicken, and Apple Salad, 12
pork:
    chops:
        Pork Chops with Sautéed
            Apples, 43
        Sunday Dutch Oven Pork, 41
    ground, Mini Turkey Meatloaves, 48
    Ham, Potato-Apple Gratin with, 64
    tenderloin, in Dressed-Up Pork
        Medallions, 39
Potato Salad with Bacon and Apples, 16
potato:
    Cabbage and Apple Soup, 36
    Full-Meal Oven Roast, 40
    Potato-Apple Gratin with Ham, 64

Red Lentil Soup with Sweet Potato
    and Apple, 31
Sunday Dutch Oven Pork, 41
Vegetable and Apple Curry, 54
Pudding with Nutmeg Cream Sauce,
    Old-Timey Apple, 102
Pumpkin-Apple Muffins, 105
Pumpkin-Apple Soup with Bacon, 26
Quesadillas with Apples & Brie, Chicken, 23
raisins:
    Apple Bread Pudding with Caramel
        Sauce, 95
    Apple-Stuffed Acorn Squash, 66
    Easy Apple Strudel, 89
    Maple Raisin-Apple Tartlets, 86
    Mini Turkey Meatloaves, 48
    Old-Timey Apple Pudding with
        Nutmeg Cream Sauce, 102
    Rhubarb-Apple Conserve, 121
    Spinach-Apple Sauté, 55
    Sweet Potato, Orange, and Apple
        Bake, 52
    Vegetable and Apple Curry, 54
Red Lentil Soup with Sweet Potato and
    Apple, 31
Rhubarb-Apple Conserve, 121

Roasted Apple-Vegetable Medley,
    Parmesan, 56
Rustic Apple Tart, 83
Sauce, Nutmeg Cream, 102
sausage:
    Apple-Link Salad, 15

Overnight Breakfast Casserole, 62
Sausage and Apple Pasta, 59
Savory Sausage-and-Apple Rice
    Stuffing, 58
Spinach-Apple Sauté, 55
Savory Sausage-and-Apple Rice
    Stuffing, 58
Slaw, Apple, 24
Slaw, Warm Five-Spice Apple, 53
Slow-Cooker Apple Butter, 123
Slow-Cooker Apple Cider Pot Roast, 42
Snappy Apple Salad, 11
Spice Cake, Apple Upside-Down, 92
spinach:
    Apple-Link Salad, 15
    Autumn Chicken Salad, 20
    Grilled Chicken, Apple, and Leek Salad, 13
    Sausage and Apple Pasta, 59
    Spinach-Apple Sauté, 55
Stir-Fried Vegetables with Hoisin, 61
Stovetop Baked Apples, 120
Stovetop Cran-Apple Cobbler, 100
Strudel, Easy Apple, 89
Stuffing, Fruity, 69
Stuffing, Savory Sausage-and-Apple
    Rice, 58
Sunday Dutch Oven Pork, 41
Sweet Potato and Apple, Red Lentil
    Soup with, 31
Sweet Potato, Orange, and Apple Bake, 52
Sweet-and-Sour Cabbage and Apple
    Skillet, 50
Tart Dough, 85
tarts and tartlets:
    Burnished-Apple Tart Ring, 84
    Maple Raisin-Apple Tartlets, 86
    Rustic Apple Tart, 83
Topping, Cinnamon Crumble, 72
Turkey Meatballs with Apple-Dijon Glaze, 47
Turkey Meatloaves, Mini, 48
turnips, in Full-Meal Oven Roast, 40
Upside-Down Spice Cake, Apple, 92
Vegetable and Apple Curry, 54
vegetable medley (broccoli, carrot, and
    cauliflower), in Pimento Cream Soup, 34
Vinaigrette, Honey Mustard, 16
Vinaigrette, Honey, 13
walnuts, in Food Processor Apple Bread, 110
Warm Five-Spice Apple Slaw, 53
white beans, in Baked Beans with Apple, 65
Wonton Apple Pockets À La Mode, 80

Metric Conversion Chart

VOLUME MEASUREMENTS		WEIGHT MEASUREMENTS		TEMPERATURE CONVERSION	
U.S.	Metric	U.S.	Metric	Fahrenheit	Celsius
1 teaspoon	5 ml	½ ounce	15 g	250	120
1 tablespoon	15 ml	1 ounce	30 g	300	150
¼ cup	60 ml	3 ounces	90 g	325	160
⅓ cup	75 ml	4 ounces	115 g	350	180
½ cup	125 ml	8 ounces	225 g	375	190
⅔ cup	150 ml	12 ounces	350 g	400	200
¾ cup	175 ml	1 pound	450 g	425	220
1 cup	250 ml	2¼ pounds	1 kg	450	230